Our Past Leaves

Our Past Leaves

Poems by

James Croal Jackson

Cover design by Shay Culligan

ISBN: 978-1-954353-96-1

Kelsay Books
502 South 1040 East, A-119
American Fork, Utah, 84003

For my family

Acknowledgments

Thanks to the following literary journals, which originally published many of these poems:

3Elements Review: "Switches"
Chronogram: "The Funeral"
Creative Writing Ink: "In Waves"
Ethel Zine: "The Persistence of Memory"
Every Writer: "Mom Recalls How Dad Used to Walk for Miles"
frak/ture: "Even in the Nostalgia of My Happiest Era"
The Green Light: "Junkyard"
Hello America Stereo Cassette: "Eyes (Mine)"
Jokes Review: "Temporary Treasures"
KGB Bar Lit Mag: "Capstone"
Kingdoms in the Wild: "Cracked Windshield"
Pirene's Fountain: "Meditation on Muscle Memory"
Pouch: "Blue Beetle"
The Road Not Taken: "Lawnmower / Guitar"
Rubbertop Review: "Clinton, Ohio"
Sampsonia Way: "Attending a Polo Match on the Ten-Year Anniversary of My Father's Death"
San Diego Poetry Annual: "Landscaping"
South Florida Poetry Journal: "Some Crimson Planet"
Subterranean Blue Poetry: "Acquaintance"
Sybil Journal: "Cape May Karaoke," "Tetris"
Vagabond City Lit: "Dream with Patchwork Moon"
Wizards in Space: "Memory"

Contents

Blue Beetle 11

Memory 13

Junkyard 15

Even in the Nostalgia of My Happiest Era 16

Dream with Patchwork Moon 17

Some Crimson Planet 18

In Waves 19

The Persistence of Memory 20

Trimming Trees 21

Cape May Karaoke 22

Tetris 23

Switches 24

Acquaintance 25

Temporary Treasures 26

Lawnmower / Guitar 28

Meditation on Muscle Memory 29

The Funeral 31

Mom Recalls How Dad Used to Walk for Miles 32

Cracked Windshield 33

Phone Conversation with My Sister on Christmas
Day 34

Landscaping 36

Capstone 37

Attending a Polo Match on the Ten-Year
Anniversary of My Father's Death 38

Clinton, Ohio 39

Eyes (Mine) 40

Blue Beetle

shining
in the sunlight
of our driveway

I go inside
to tell Dad

come see
what
I
found

no hesitation:
he squishes
its golden
guts out

a thing like
that

he says

is nothing
more
than a nuisance

but I keep
thinking
about that beetle

impossibly one
of a kind

and today
I watched
a boring

black
beetle

scurry
across
the pavement
of Goodale Park

and disappear
into grass

and I thought

the ground
is teeming
with beetles

if I just dig
a hole
deep enough

I might
be able
to apologize

Memory

Inconsequential things I remember—
each World Series winner
of the past forty years or, say,
brushing my teeth last month, blood
in my spit, then finding the measured
infinity of my eyes in the mirror.

I forget most things about my father
most days.

Sure. I remember
the gray-red beard,
his crooked back, faded jeans.
The freshwater scent of Polo Blue.
And those brown, gentle eyes—
but his voice?

Mixture of sediment and tire
smoke rising from gravel,
a '55 Ford Thunderbird fading from view.

I started journaling to remember better
but now write poems under the dim lamp on my desk.

(Years later, you know which
one. Gold, bendable neck. A thrift store.
But you're still no good
with the finer details.)

A waterfall of my father. Illusions
of life doodle-sketched
in some spacey lobe of my mind.

I wonder: do I give myself enough
credit? What's worth remembering?

I am inside a coffee shop, writing,
surrounded by people I won't recall.

I look for a subject. A gray, old man sits
on the patio with book and beagle
yet never goes inside to buy anything.

I pay for him. I pay him
in remembering.

Junkyard

I grew up with a yard full of worthless
a ministry of rare Earth metals   there was
a patch of grass to sometimes lay in
I'd reflect the sun   never photosynthesizing
there is an unwell that swells in me whenever
I go home to Akron   the gunsmoke clouds
always gathered above where the rabid dogs
would bark   & I was raised beside inoperable
cars   my father cranking the crowbar lug nuts
of too many punctured tires   no spares unused
a basement of bolts and lubricants   white bottled
Dad spoke mechanics to me incomprehensible
tongue   until a tire burst on a dead stretch
of highway the other day   I had to pull over
and recall the broken way he explained things

Even in the Nostalgia of My Happiest Era

I think of the lawn, the grass I had
to cut by the mouthfuls, sink into
something other than summer, the flesh
of work, beer bottles piling in the margins
of the yard. I'd take my gloves off—hungover
July—to pick up last night's blurry harmonicas.
Oh, I'd sing the songs through my teeth.
I lapped at youth forever cranking the tracks
from *Myth,* the blue days buzzing
by. Granny apples were rotting
in the yard beneath my nose. Even then
I told myself *I can't stay here forever.*

Dream with Patchwork Moon

My love, I want to show you this strange moon:
a quilted wine and blue, half the charcoal sky—
but you are playing a game, a Crash Bandicoot

offshoot where you are a humanoid frog who jumps
and spins across 3-D landscapes. I ask you *please
come outside there is a nervous crowd gathering*

for this cosmic anomaly. But no one dies because
I wake and recall my childhood summers spent
on the cold, brown, teddy bear carpet of my basement,

hands on controller, eyes mesmerized by polygons.
My father would slowly descend the stairs then ask
me to walk with him—as he often did the last

years of his life—that there was a whole world
out there, *the* world, and if I would walk once
with him he would show me, *please,* just once.

Some Crimson Planet

When I am lonely,
it helps to not think
of the universe. I imagine

Earth buried in the darkest
cemetery, a headstone
with some space separating

it from the next.
I know there must be a
tenderness quotient

in the cosmos, a rose
on some crimson planet
blooming tall to wave

at me, its petals drifting
aimlessly through
a garden of light-

years. This distance
is more collective
than we know.

In Waves

It comes in waves, the grief, though you laugh
as you say so, because we are in the Atlantic,
children again, uppercutting large tides,
and I never learned to swim, but the saying—
the metaphor—is true, the water is relentless,
and we were states away from the hospital,
where your father was, when you got the
call, and later, in our hotel's game room,
there was a balancing act—you, your family,
the ping-pong paddles on the black table,
the plastic balls rolling slowly onto the floor
at the end of another meaningless set, the
bouncing, then physics, entropy ending—
how else to reconcile lost time? This dusting,
this airing out, now, swimsuits soaked from
the salt of the sea, this fabric, this residue
dripping off of this vacation into the old
Civic, the broken A/C, the windows' open
breeze, silence of the road lodged between
green hills, so endless, our breathing.

The Persistence of Memory

Salvador Dali
liked his spaghetti
soft as can

be: drooping
off the plate.

But Dad always
said *stop playing
with your food!*

I wish I could
have figured it out
before he died. I

would have told
him I was toying
with time.

Trimming Trees

When my father retired, he could not end
the work—sunrise blurred to sunset
sculpting trees within the canvas of our yard.
S*oon,* he said, *you will wear my work
on your hands.* But after he passed, my hands
would tremble leaning ladder onto tree,
snipping branches off the living
limbs.

Cape May Karaoke

vocals rise night static the beach house we
sway to midi music   call ourselves karaoke

machines   what disappointment   to not be
whole   humid June   familiar shadows

encroach the move I crack my song an egg
to thee   to thaw cold exhibitions of the

bottle another   popped Corona to thirst
for grand experiences   cheaply   the tide

a tape loop   I do not sing the steady
hand of a lyric   but rather the water

Tetris

I am reading old journals, putting
pieces of my past in place—
a series of staircase Tetris shapes,

a broken board mixing L.A. palm
fronds with bad haircuts Dad
gave me, but we needed to save

money, and I was bratty. I wanted
video game anime hair but got slanted
bangs laughed at by classmates and

teachers (who would never admit they
found it funny). I knew, and still do.
Sharp laughter edged in memory. I

want to say I've gotten over it. Over
all of it. But I still hold the smoky
gray of Nintendo controller in both

hands, and I am trying to tell the pieces
where they need to go—but I am
older and life is faster, blocks falling

into places I can no longer find them,
stacking dark spaces to the top of my
screen after these earlier, easier years.

Switches

Dad knew which fuse box switch did what—
in this way, he chose for us the light and dark.
His hands blackened from cracking walnuts
over the years, hammering husks in the

night when the rest of us were sleeping,
loud whacks startling us temporarily awake then
drifting back into our own darknesses beneath familiar
stars. After his death, we found Dad's walnuts

in barrels in the corner of his workshop alongside
spiders and memories we could not yet scrape.
My brother said, to honor him, we had to break
and eat each one, despite the bulk. That Dad lived

a rich life poor, that the taste might activate
memory's accordion, careening us in and out
of past and present, turning life to death then life
again, discordant in its forlorn loudness.

Acquaintance

I know nothing
about you anymore.
Can't remember conversations.

Sometimes you are a leaf
blowing past the yard of memory,
a whisper likening

myself to wind.

Temporary Treasures

my father once mowed a rabbit into the lawn—
perfection leaves corpses

the tractor drones loud radio static

I never want to be someone
who compares pop music
to a limping tornado

autumn's kaleidoscope leaves
the crumpled xylophone

black bags the scattered records

a taut-needled march to old age
I say these things now
but Eugene Delacroix said it best:

he was like a man owning a piece of ground
in which, unknown to himself, a treasure lay buried

music of the ether
of shifting chatter
fang-laughs from the teenage zeitgeist

when else has our unity
hinged on the city's mustard smell

whether it's there
or there isn't

vapidity is DNA's rapt curse
relinquishing joyrides for dimes
is our chosen profession

I prefer cremation to cream
and commitment to half & half

ambulances shriek when people talk
I never hear the atmosphere's shrill
nor slow warmth of glaciers

in the spring of mottled souls
what is that frozen world?

we should unearth its hardened treasures

Lawnmower / Guitar

Lawnmower string / guitar heart—
pull, strum, start then stop the song.
It's dead grass. Its broken neck.
B-chord specks. Shades of saffron.

It's dandelion season—
one reason to sing with blades.
Grass frets yet begins anew.
Rotors drone through spring. Charades.

Meditation on Muscle Memory

If I had musical talent
I might not write poems.

Guitar-grown fingernails.
Nimble strings.

There's no need
to lie. I couldn't bring myself to try

when my parents thought
it'd be a good idea for me
to take piano lessons.

I had Game Boy eyes
and the Final Fantasy theme on repeat.

My dad had already explained
the difference between basin wrench

and torque. Wasted an afternoon
taping leaking pipes.

Like many of his time
he knew plumbing, mechanics,
home improvement

then brought me into rooms with broken
machines. My mind was Mickey Mouse
spelling words and song,

not the kind to vivisect
a bird to learn the function.

All I knew was not yet
and still my hands
sing few callouses.

The Funeral

After Band of Horses

After my sister's morning call broke
our father's death, the first thing

I did was listen to *Everything All the Time,*
sobbing into unrequited guitar

and an ethereal voice soaring
into some great beyond. Seven years later,

I drink Bordeaux with my roommate
in the kitchen, cyclical tones

filling the room. The guitar is a coffin
for us both, lowering Dad's corpse

into dirt. Her grandpa died
when this song released.

We rake our past leaves under burnt-out bulbs.
We agree: *The Funeral* was written for both of us

to pass each billionth insignificant day.
Dead leaves own the lawn each season

of our funerals. The same deaths
in autumn chill still dropping the needle

into memory's vinyl—to come up only
to pull us under, show us wrong.

Mom Recalls How Dad Used to Walk for Miles

In those wild woods, poison sumac
would distance one from active tracks—
jagged moan, trembling steel, cerulean sky
waiting for your call: an endless horizon,
a warbler singing quietly
into night.

Cracked Windshield

Sudden the stone that cracked
the windshield, the storm that
struck the heirloom oak—you
ask for rain, beg for answers.
Soaked hands steer through
the blindness of the blur—
ten years now since Dad
merged into the final lane,
his pass misjudging distance
from collision, and that night
Mom heard a screeching
in her bedroom like a crow
passing from another world,
a bleak siren thrusting her
to darkness her headlights
could not cut through.

Phone Conversation with My Sister on Christmas Day

The trees are dead, she said.
Peering outside, it was true:
a still-barren sixty degrees, sun
meekly reveling in its new warm.

A week ago, our mother cut down the tree
we picked apples from as children.
They were small, red, never delicious—
brown and burrowed with worms

because anything sweet from the skin
isn't as sweet as you might think.
All those colorful lights we tied around
the necks of plastic and decoration,

the way we choked the holiday,
wrung out the last ounces of life
from the pines' animal ornaments:
the walrus with the broken tusk,

the hyena whose laugh we can
hear. As if anthropomorphizing could
ever atone for the past but I would love
to believe in a world where a fragment of

a tusk means something is truly missing—
perhaps rickety laughter ringing through
thin walls, dominant as the wooden organ
moans his mantra: *everything in this world*

is connected. Not every connected thing
is aware of its living, its connection.
But the way fingers dance deep
resonance out of the organ's shifty teeth

to provide holiness for the changed house
is the gift we must open for ourselves
with our hands full of music—a sourness
in harmony, an ode to shriveled apples.

Landscaping

Bug guts in red shed—
backyard. Dad had
clippers with my name
engraved. I didn't
trim trees after death.
Hired hands, tired
hands, ceramic
sculptured lawn.
I had to leave.
Family said they'd
handle the rest.

Capstone

among the blue desks was a meager
audition for adulthood crumpled

into a mess of wooden shadows reciting
barbell lines on the film school second

floor (stair steps closer to Orion) how
I was dreaming young of the world's

grand magnanimousness suffused
with balloons that smelled of palm frond

everglades my school-sanctioned camera
would record the nightglow trees by lights

of Coe Lake where it snowed pine cones
in the backyard of my mother's house

where acres stretch forever rugs of green grass
and hunger the endless hunger for somewhere

anywhere else

Attending a Polo Match on the Ten-Year Anniversary of My Father's Death

Death is in the shriveled blue and purple
hydrangea bouquet I gifted you. Kathy
bought the same, smaller, but they did not last
so much as linger. Mom calls me from Macy's—
where she has sold colognes for thirty years—
and says she still struggles. But, on the phone,
I am drunk on a beach towel in a horse cemetery
where Juan Carlos and his team of red ride in
circles over forgotten bones, chasing a ghost-
white ball with a mallet through the empty space
between goalposts. In the first chukker, my sister—
who broke the news I somehow already knew
with a call in the dark of a dorm room—texts
me that she's thinking of me today. At halftime,
when spectators are invited to flatten divots
on the field with their shoes, Kathy leaves
to help her family move, and the moment
she reverses her car from our tailgating spot,
I answer a call I am unaware of from my other
sister before seeing her text ask if I am okay,
that it sounded like I was in an accident
and drove into grass. No, I tell her, I am day-
drunk among ponies in the withering days
of summer. But what I don't tell her is
on the way here, Kathy didn't see the turquoise
minivan she nearly plunged into, and all we could
do as passengers was clutch the leather beneath
us as she sped full-throttle on thin and curvy roads
through the woods. We prayed to whatever tree
was nearest—birches in a blur—prayed the whole
forest to remind us that we are, briefly, breathing.

Clinton, Ohio

Where I lived was a quiet crescendo
of snow six months of the year
& mosquito summers wearing shorts
into the sweating night

Where I lived had piano thunderstorm concertos
jolting the elderly house's bones
with frenetic fingers, ivory paint,
red bricks

Where I lived was a lonesome walking trail
where morning chirps of blue jays went unnoticed.
Beds of acorns lined the autumn grass,
a kind of fallout for the process of aging
and the act of leaving

Always, now, in thought, it is a shoebox
of dandelions that writhe when I pet the cold cardboard—
hello, you are home, tonsils—my heart
can't handle the hand-shaped imprints
from so far away

Eyes (Mine)

If I tried to count how many nights I've wandered
alone to find myself, it would be on more fingers
than all my family has. If I were worried
only about eyes on walks stalking me—
if I hadn't watched The Lion
King at seven, and my father hadn't died,
and my brother—I wouldn't be present
in this field of wild cleavers with my Mufasas
whispering weeds in the moonlight. Always
that breeze tickling the hairs across
my skin. That's why I don't walk
barefoot in the grass—I don't trust strangers'
hands, so I count tendrils on everything green
in the dark that's growing, wondering
if you remember how long it took
for me to learn to tie my shoes. The laces
multiplied in my field of math
I fumbled over. My hands, I could
never be precise enough to be
a mechanic, or a surgeon.
We were in the basement and
oh, you were so patient,
television glowing and muted. Dark
news and wave band static. These
negative film reels roll to nights
embedded in memory when I try
to sleep, when my lids are full
of images. I can't believe I've stared
at the surface of the moon so many nights
over the years and just now saw
there is your face. My face.

About the Author

James Croal Jackson is a Filipino-American poet from New Franklin, Ohio. His first chapbook, *The Frayed Edge of Memory,* was published in 2017 through Writing Knights Press. His poems have appeared in hundreds of literary journals. He edits *The Mantle Poetry* and works in film production in Pittsburgh, Pennsylvania.

jamescroaljackson.com

Made in the USA
Middletown, DE
19 October 2021